AF255482

Written and Illustrated by
Takeya Trayer
TakeYaArt.com
Copyright © 2021

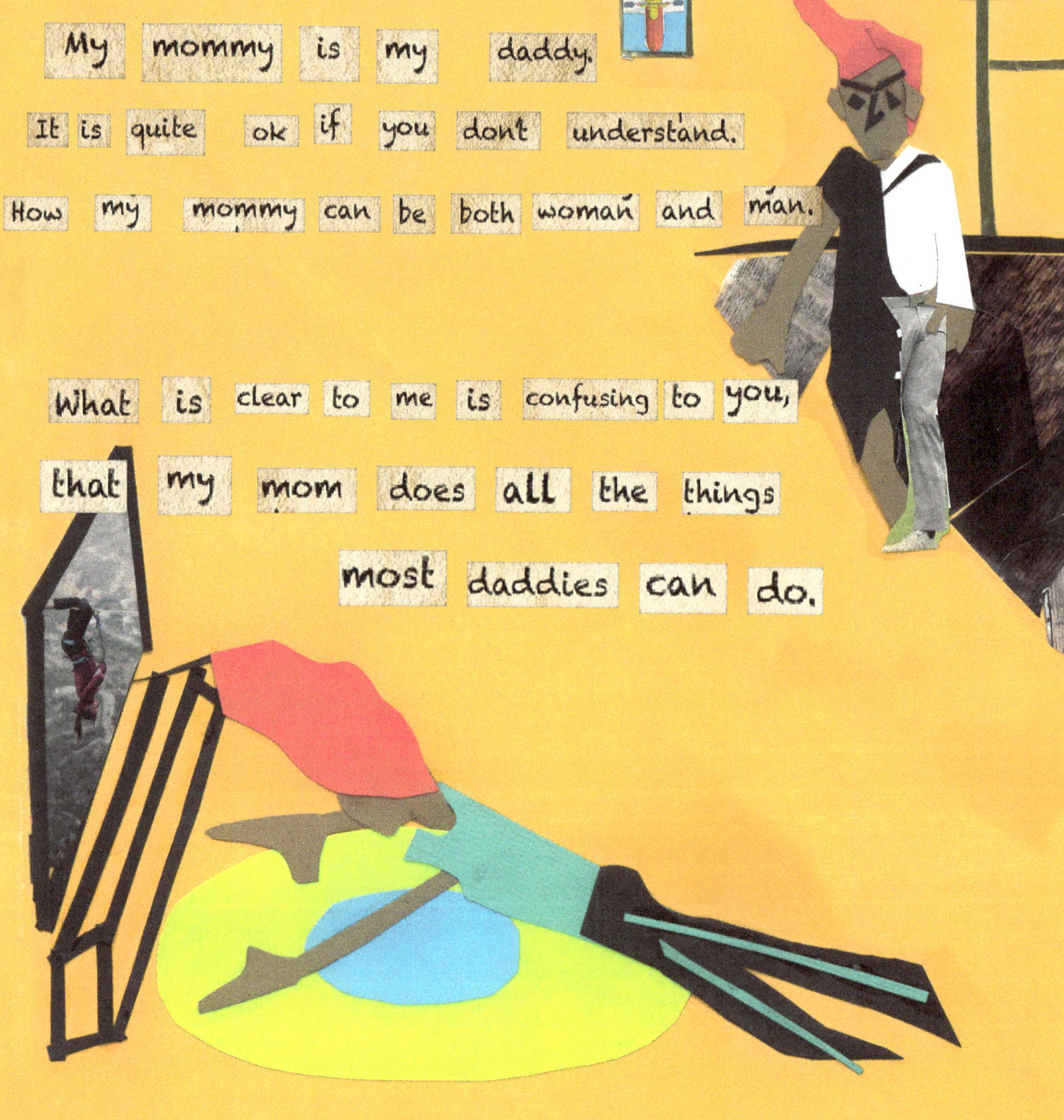
My mommy is my daddy.
It is quite ok if you dont understand.
How my mommy can be both woman and man.

What is clear to me is confusing to you,
that my mom does all the things
most daddies can do.

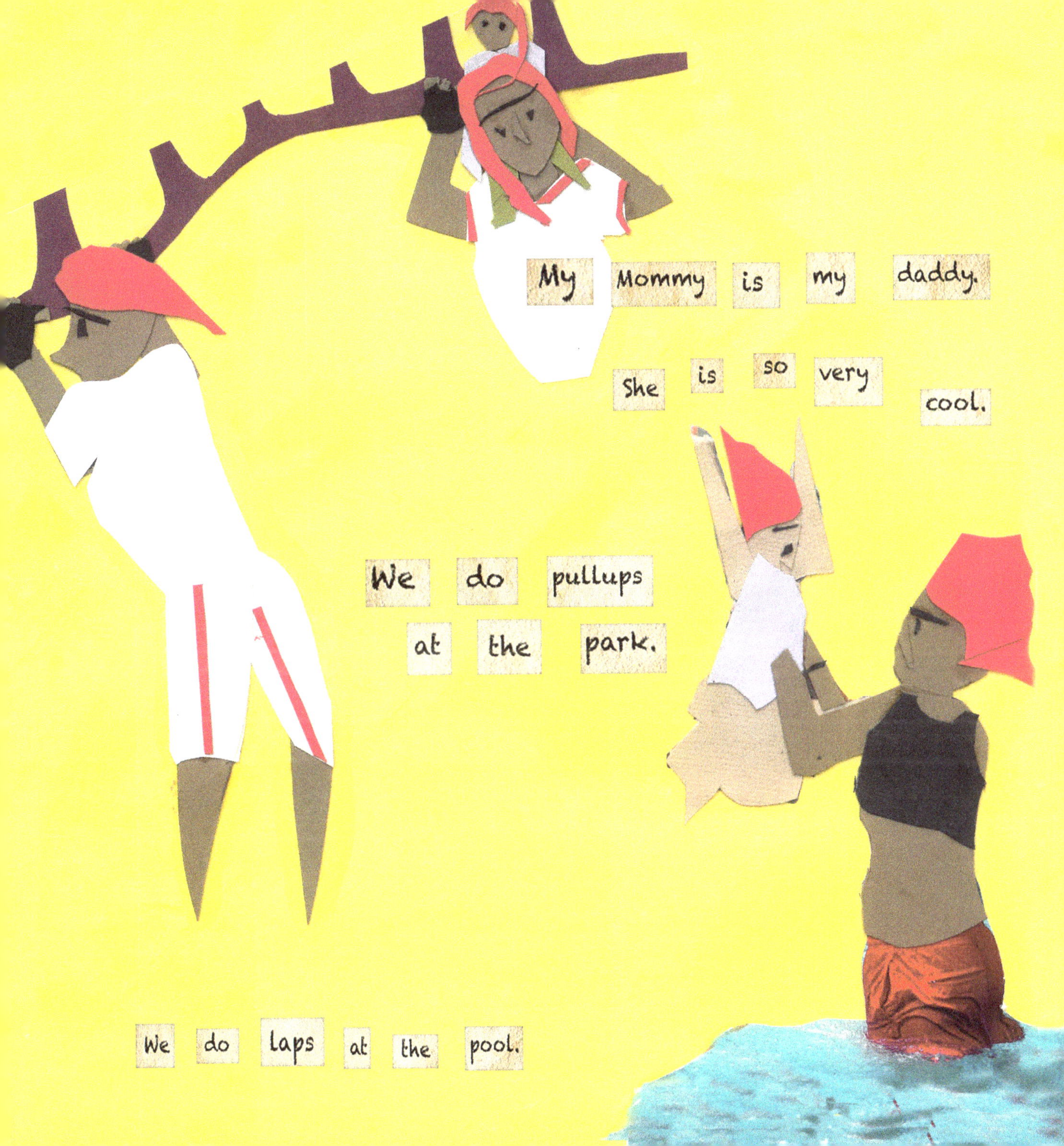

My Mommy is my daddy.
She is so very cool.
We do pullups at the park.
We do laps at the pool.

54
04
Keep Off

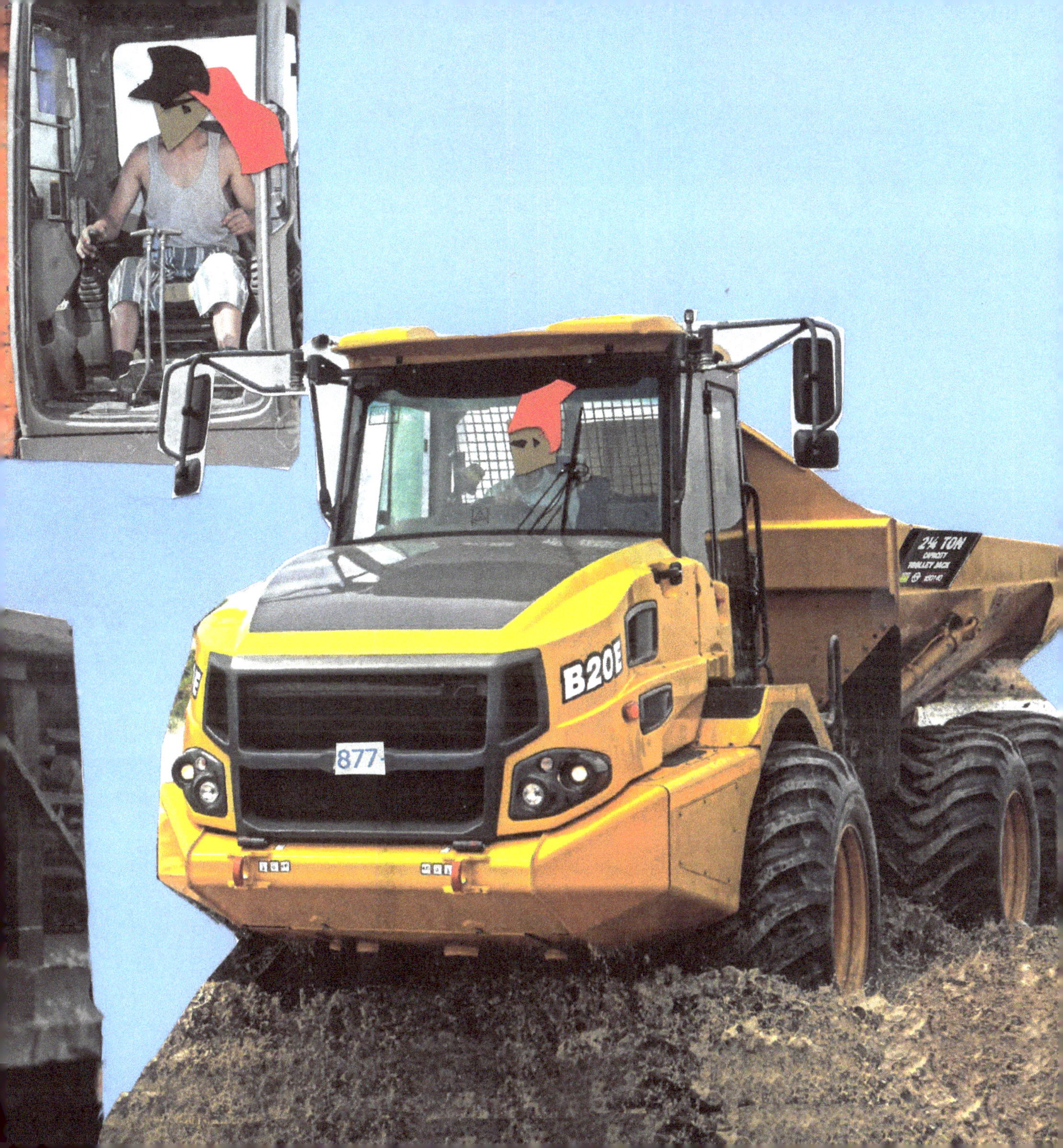

B20E
877-
2¼ TON
CAPACITY
TROLLEY JACK

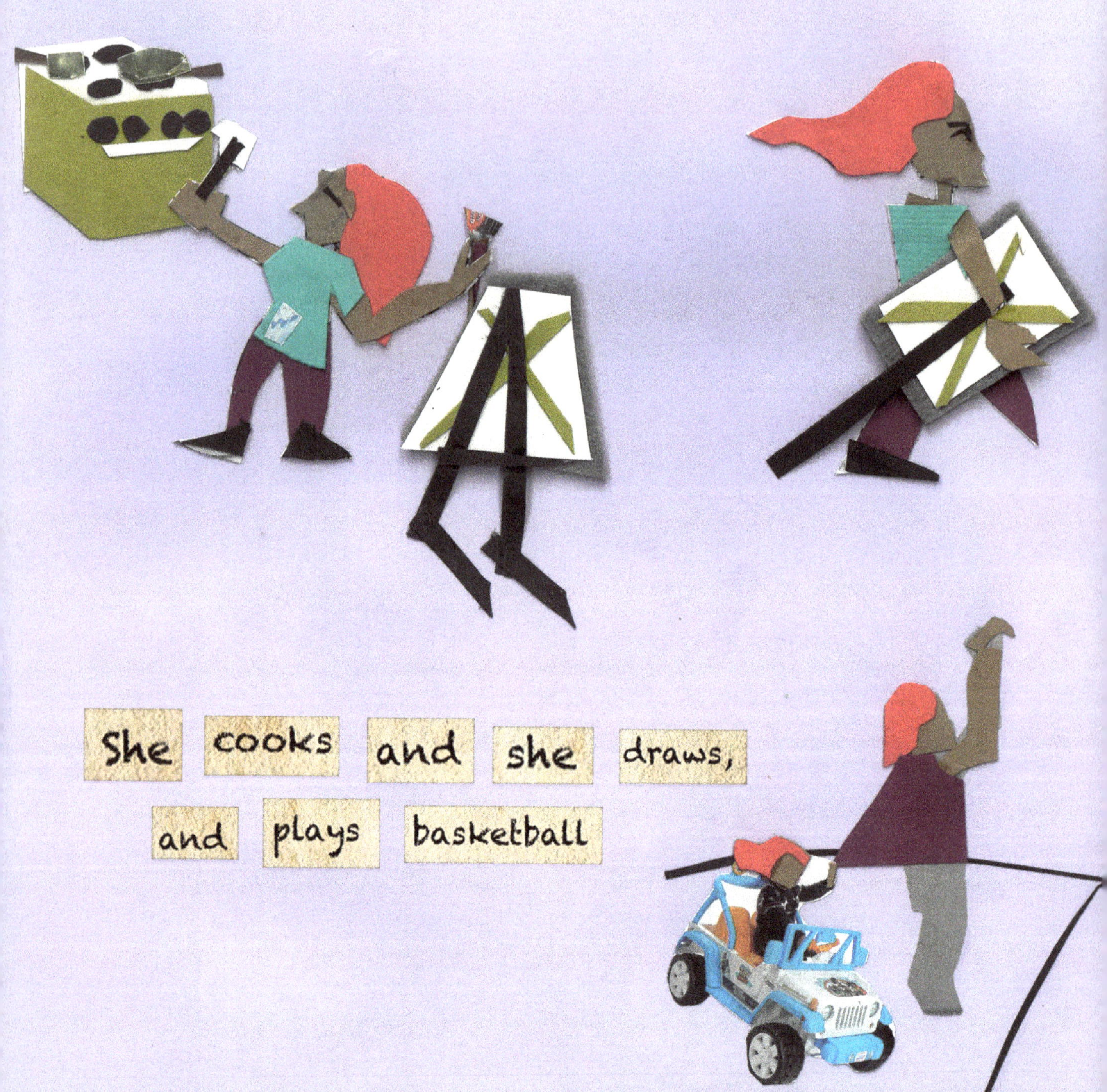

She cooks and she draws,
and plays basketball

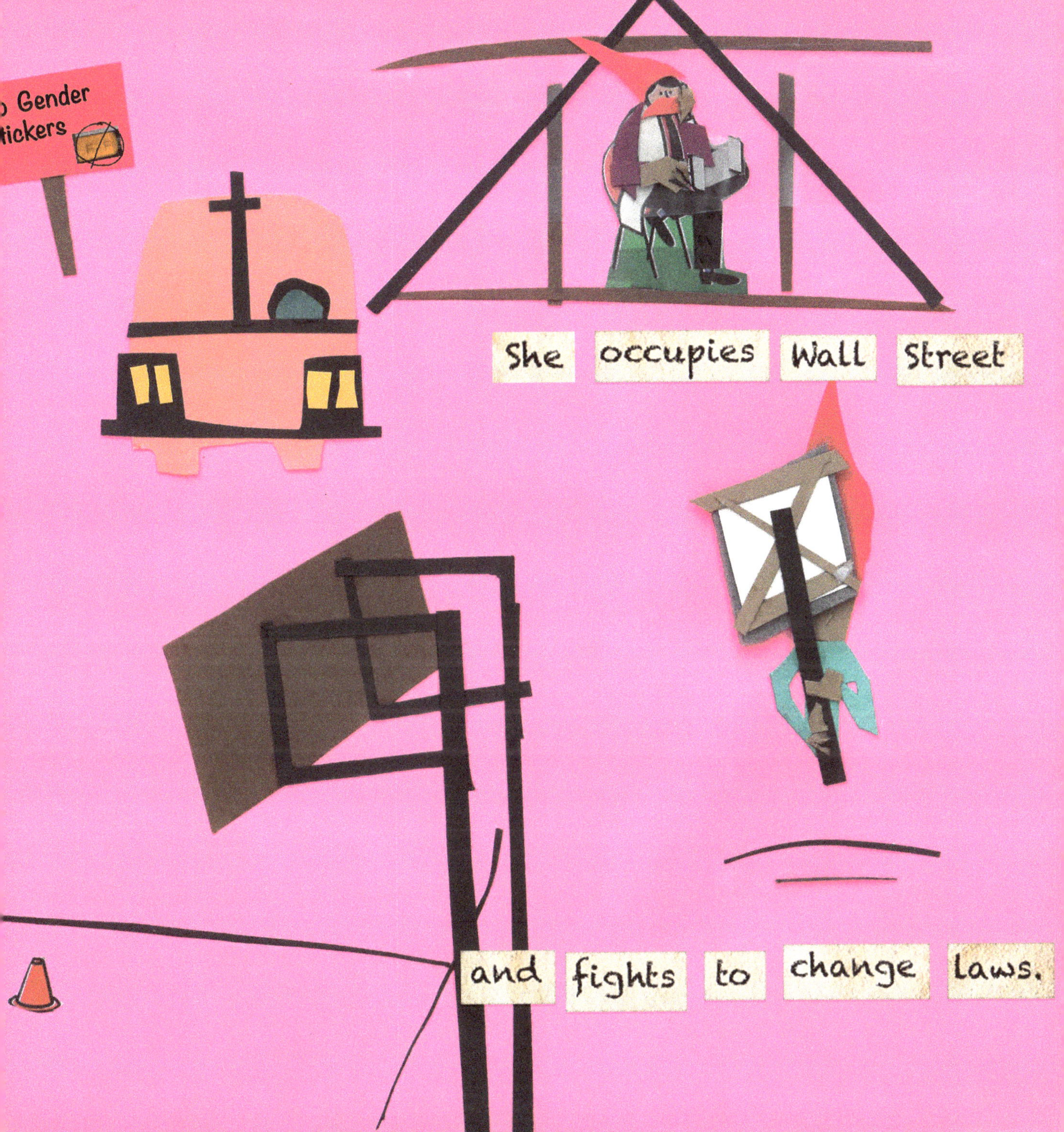
Gender
Stickers
She occupies Wall Street
and fights to change laws.

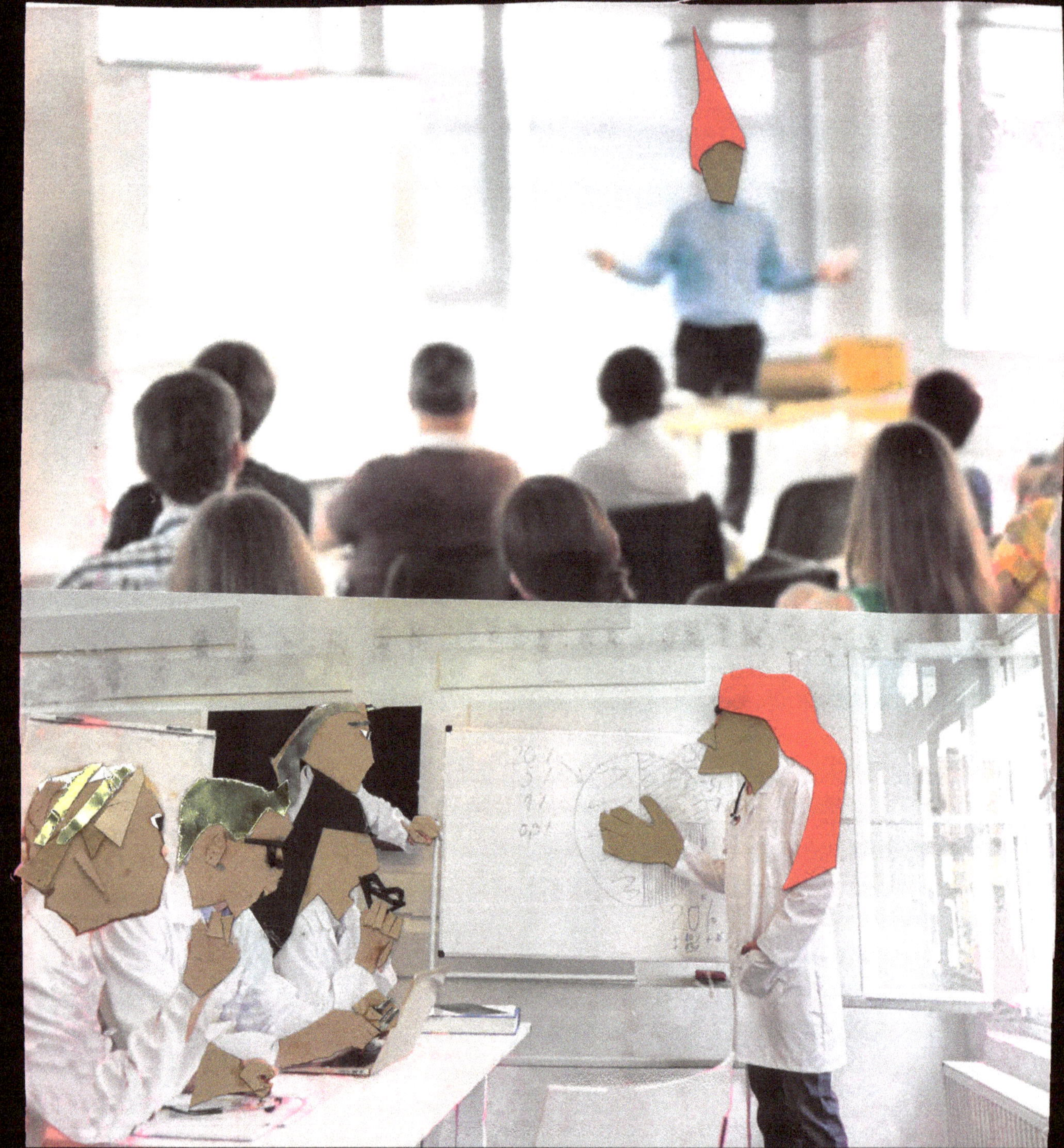

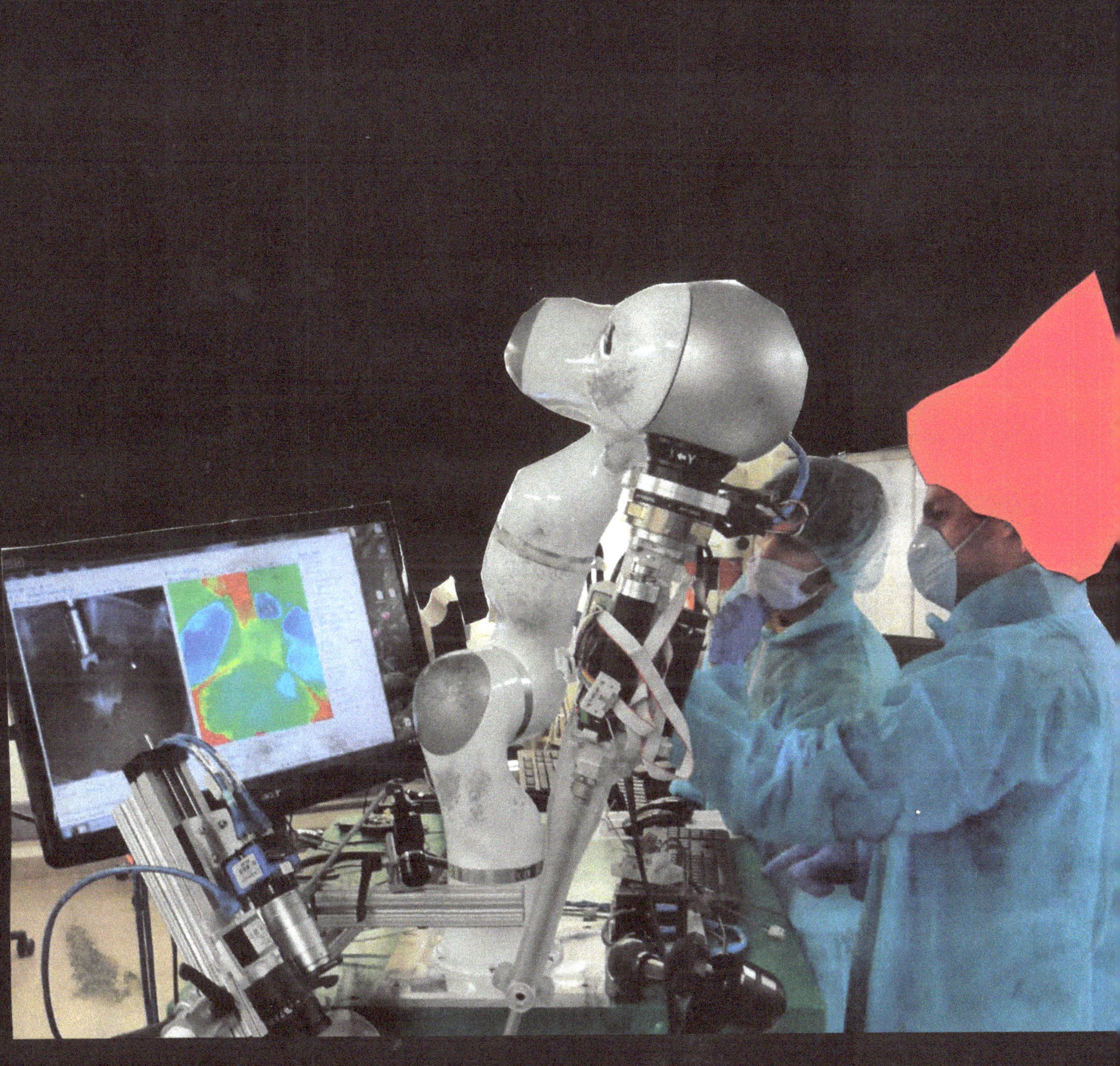

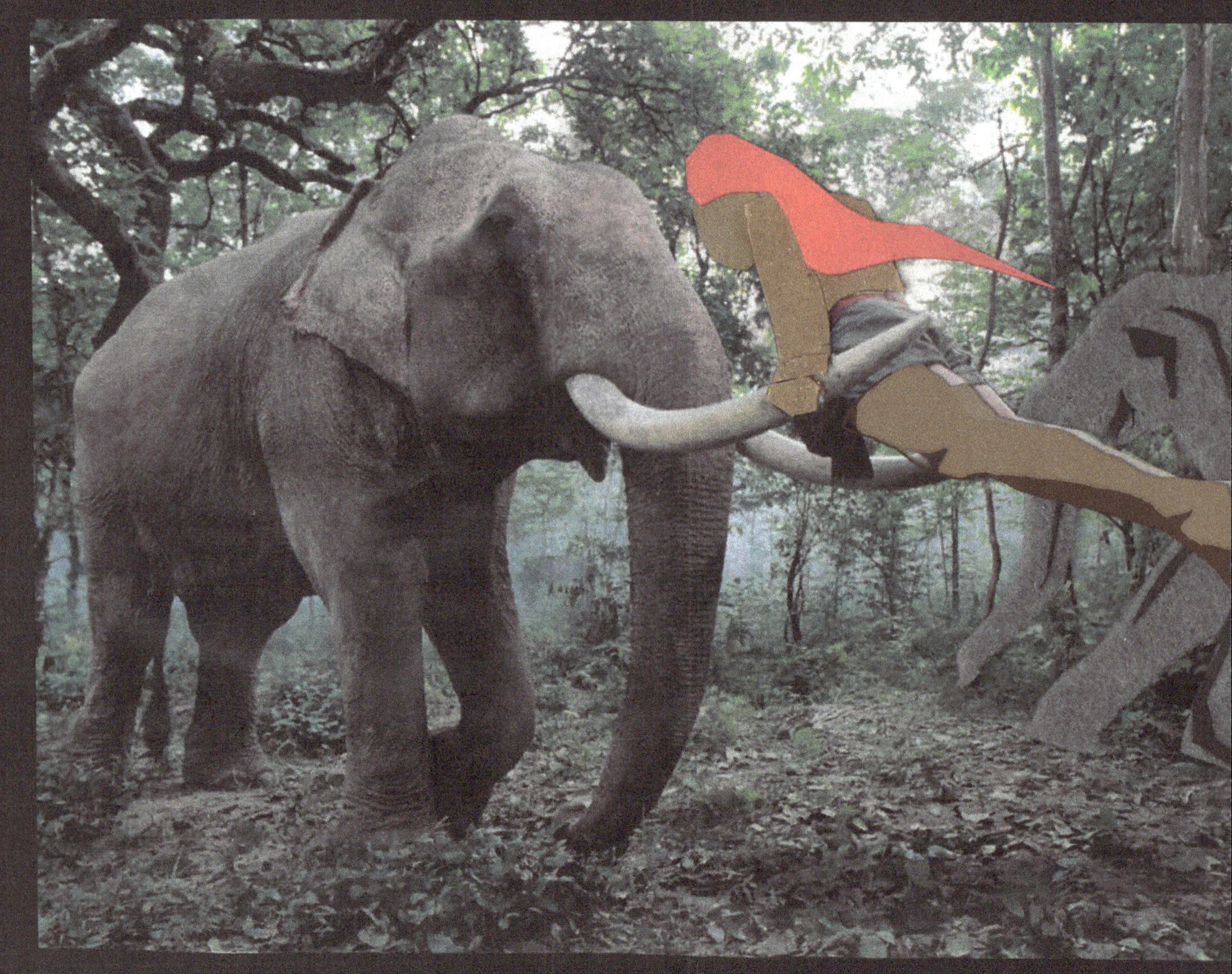

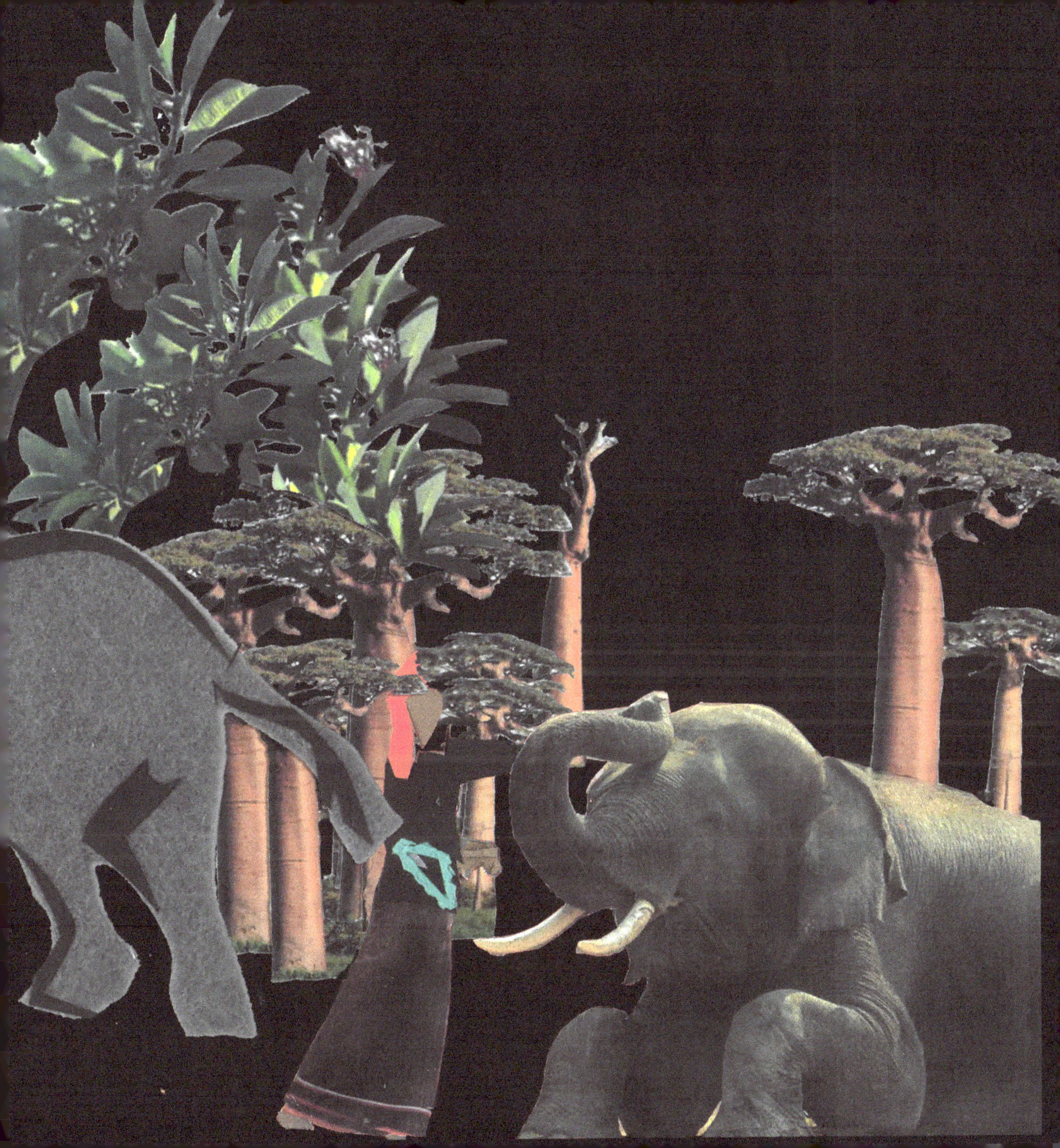

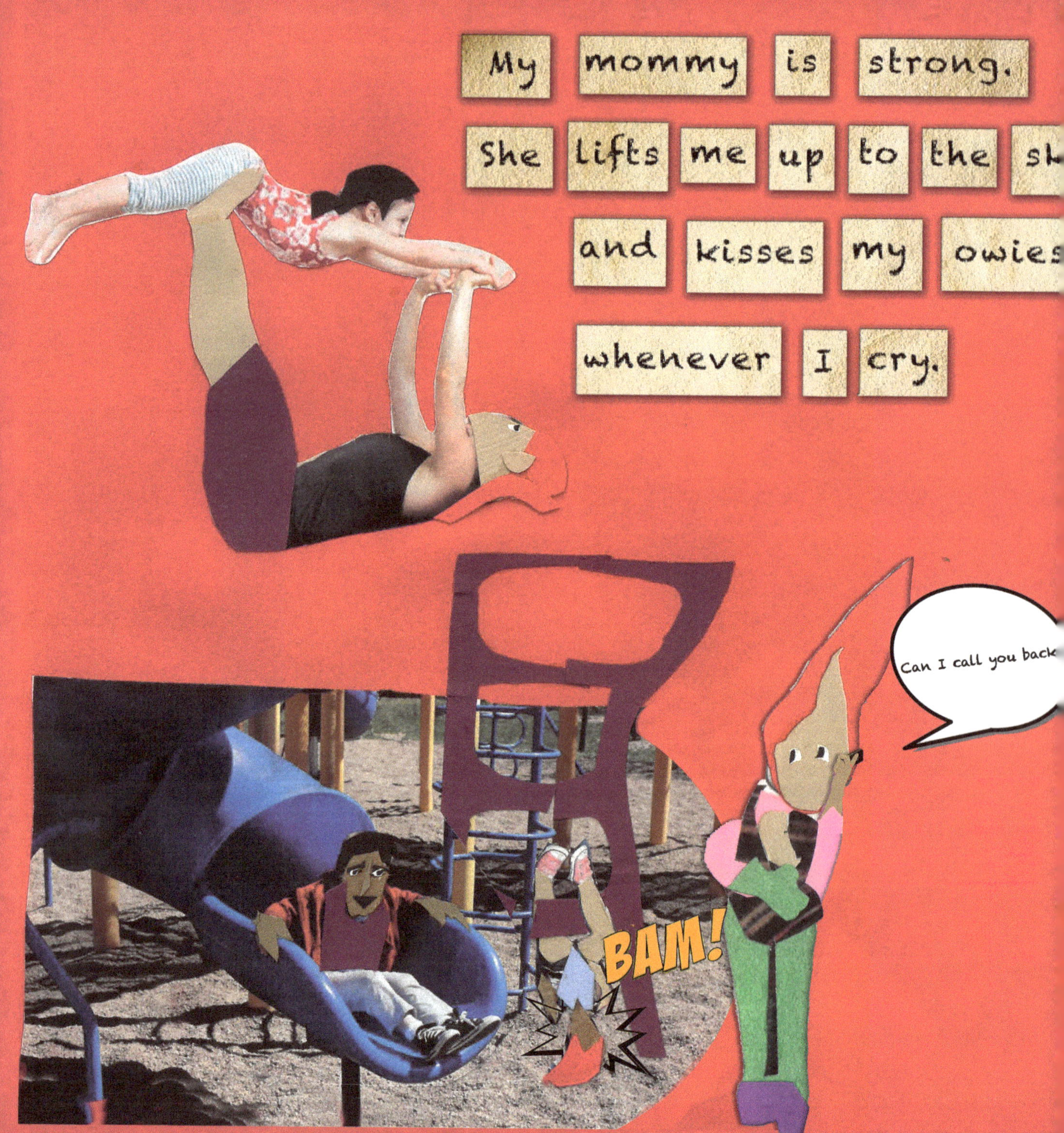

My mommy is strong. She lifts me up to the sk[y]
and kisses my owies whenever I cry.
Can I call you back
BAM!

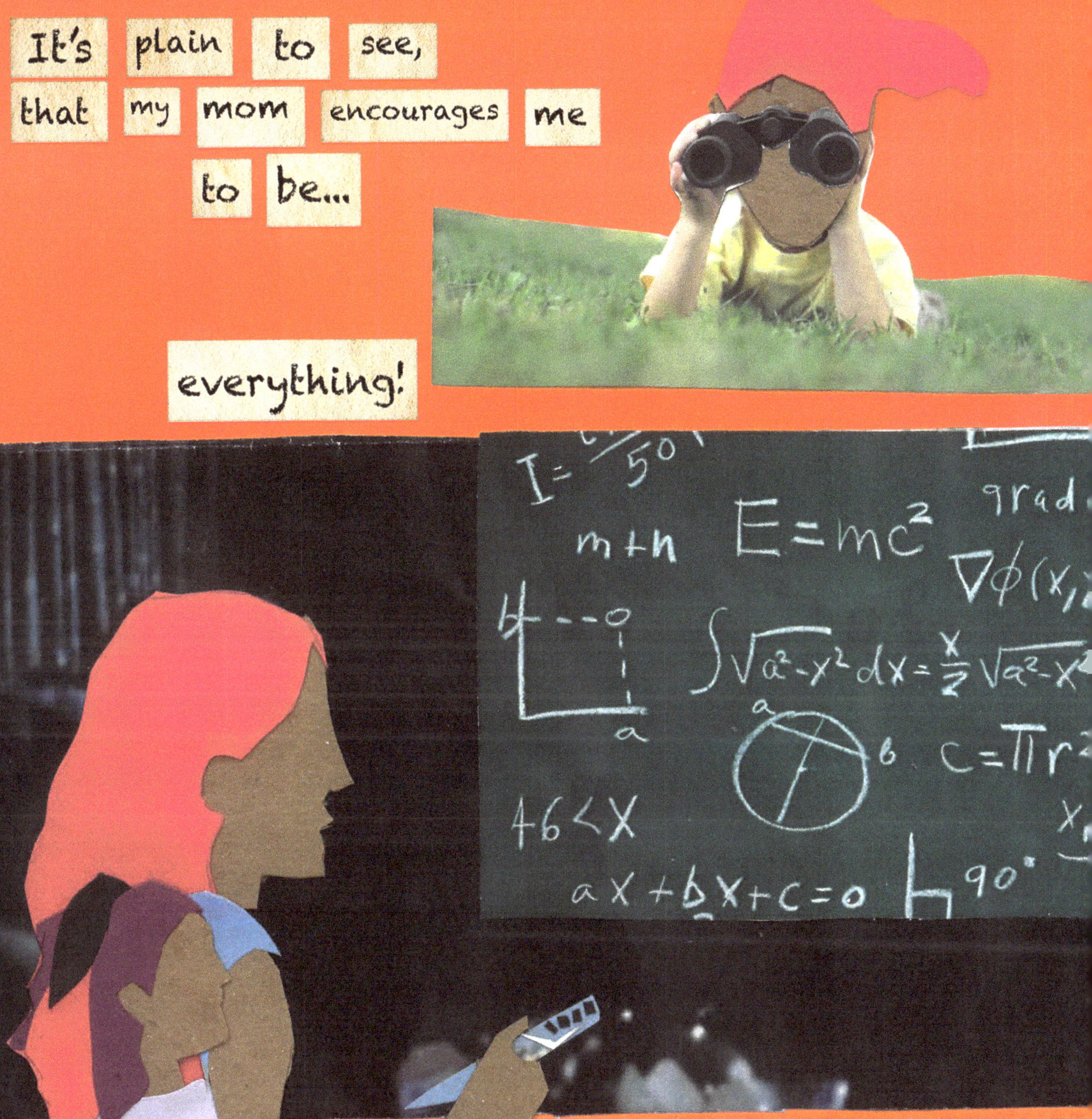
It's plain to see,
that my mom encourages me
to be...
everything!
E=mc²

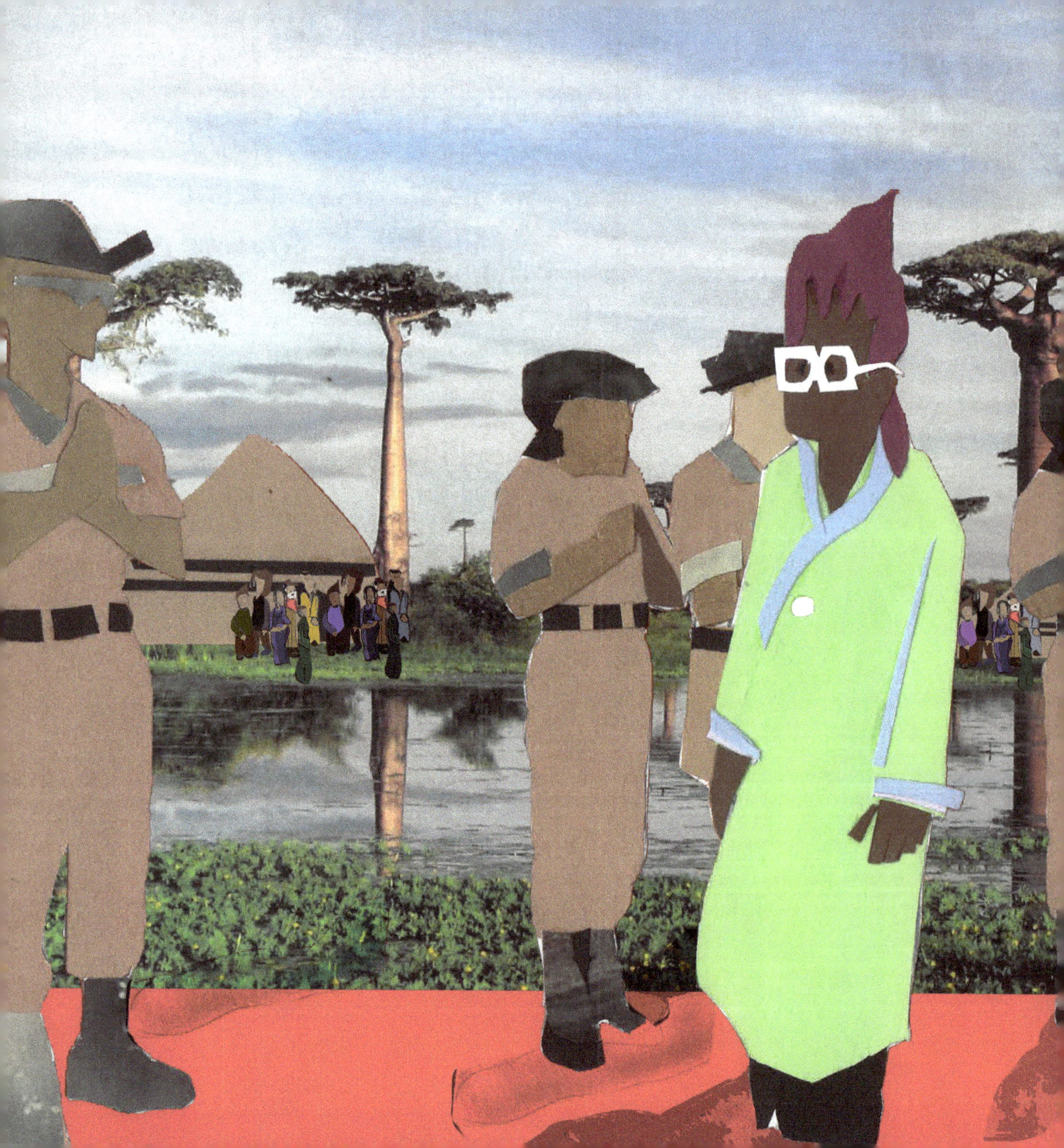

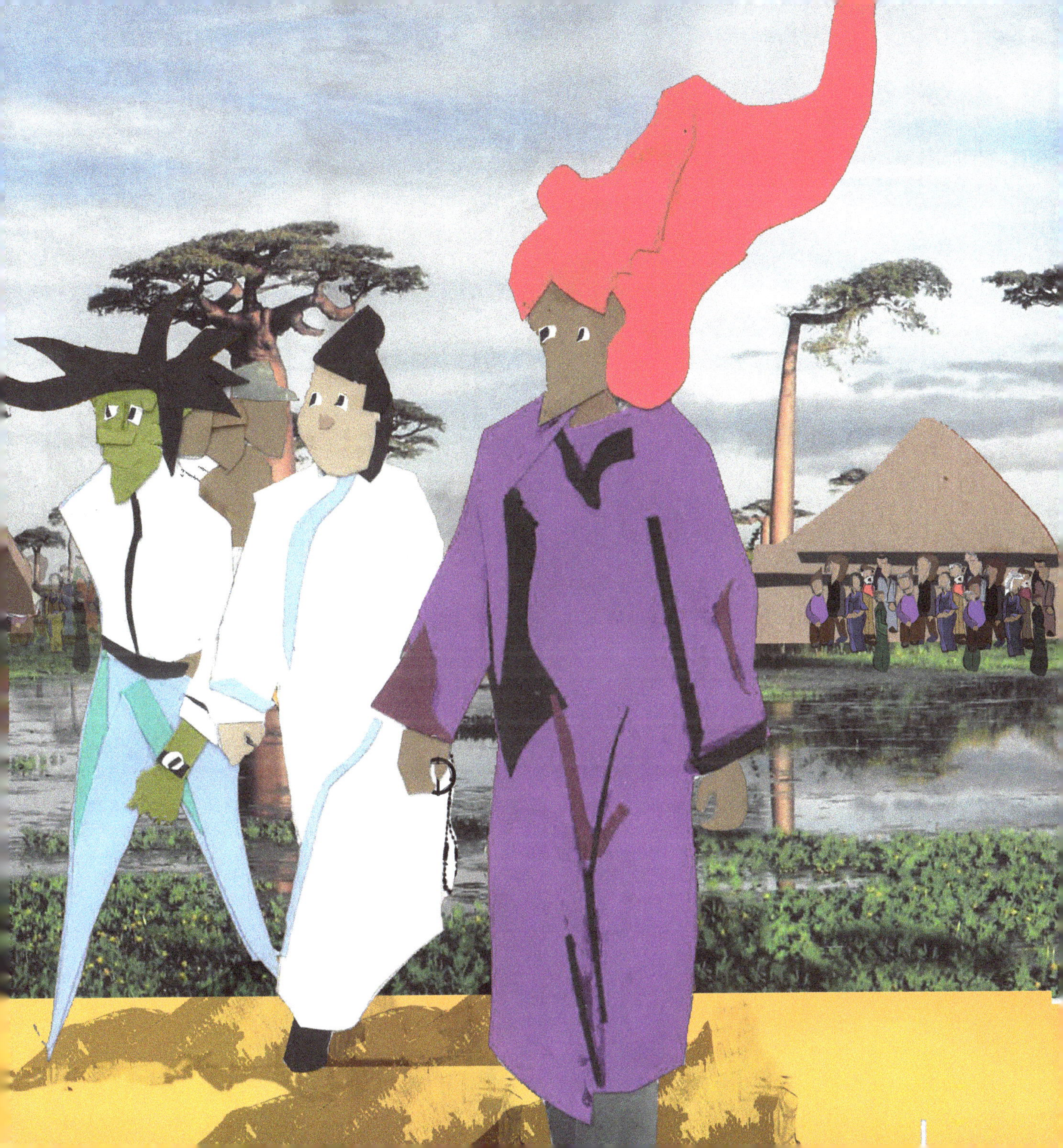

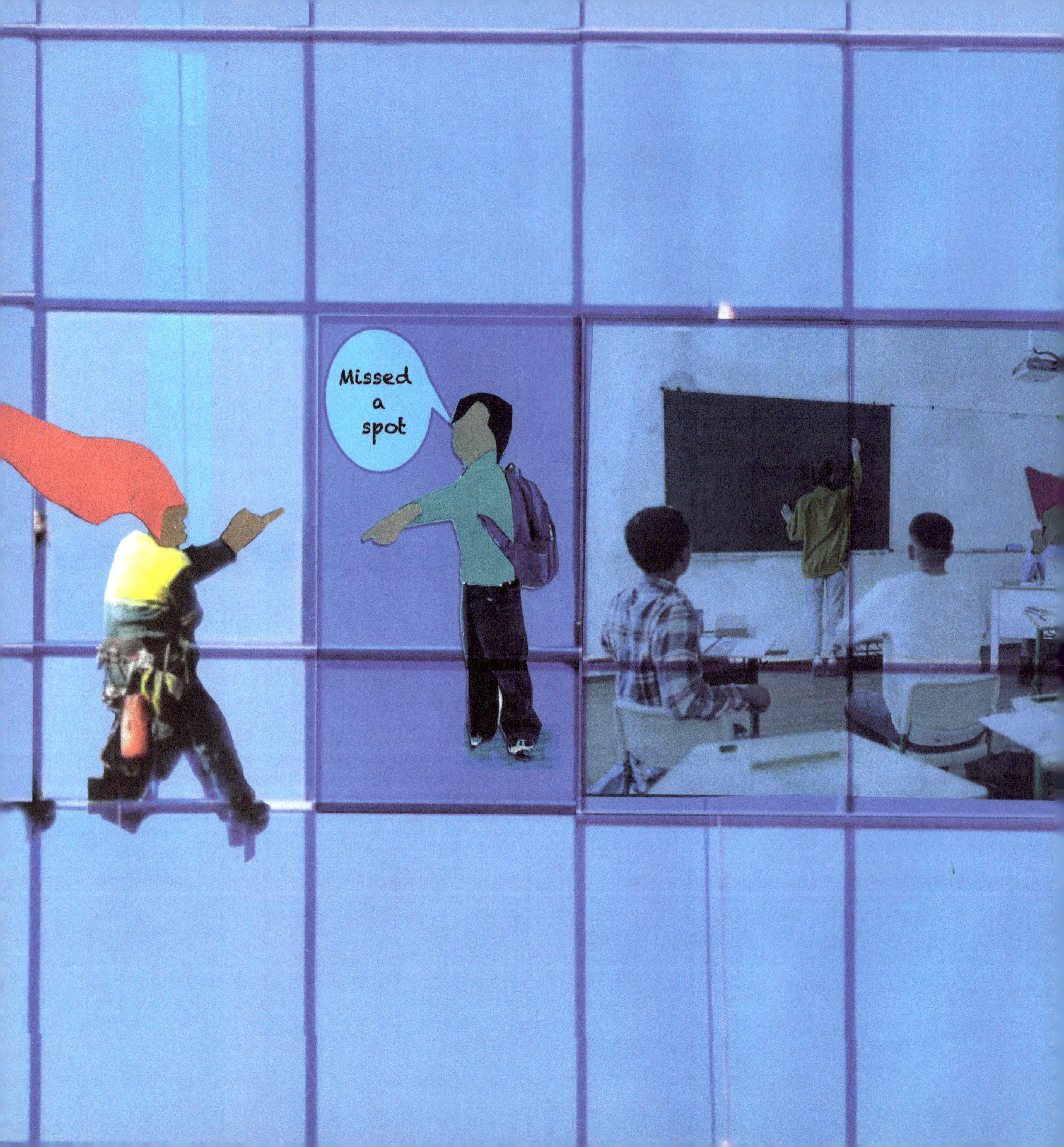
Missed
a
spot

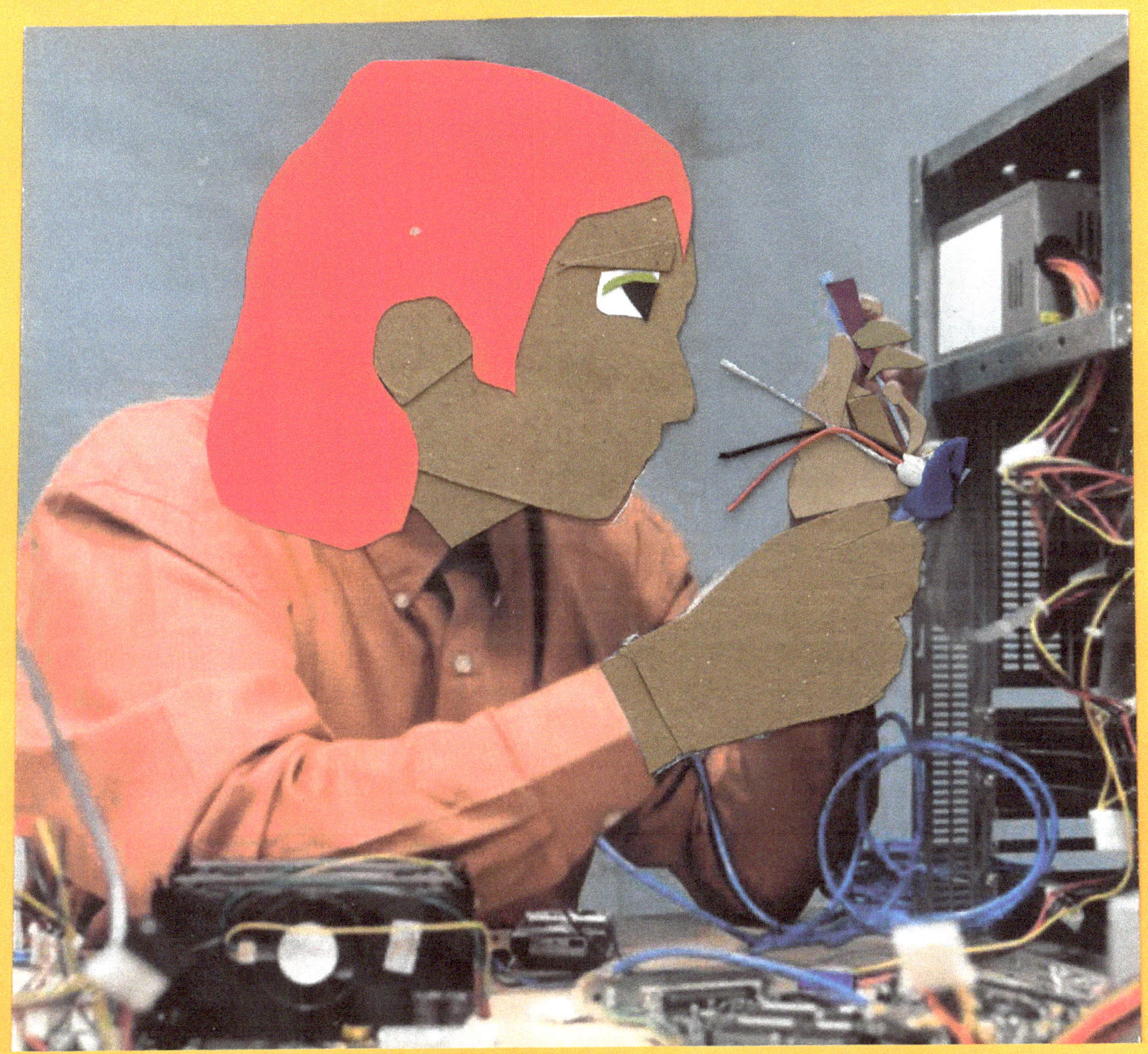

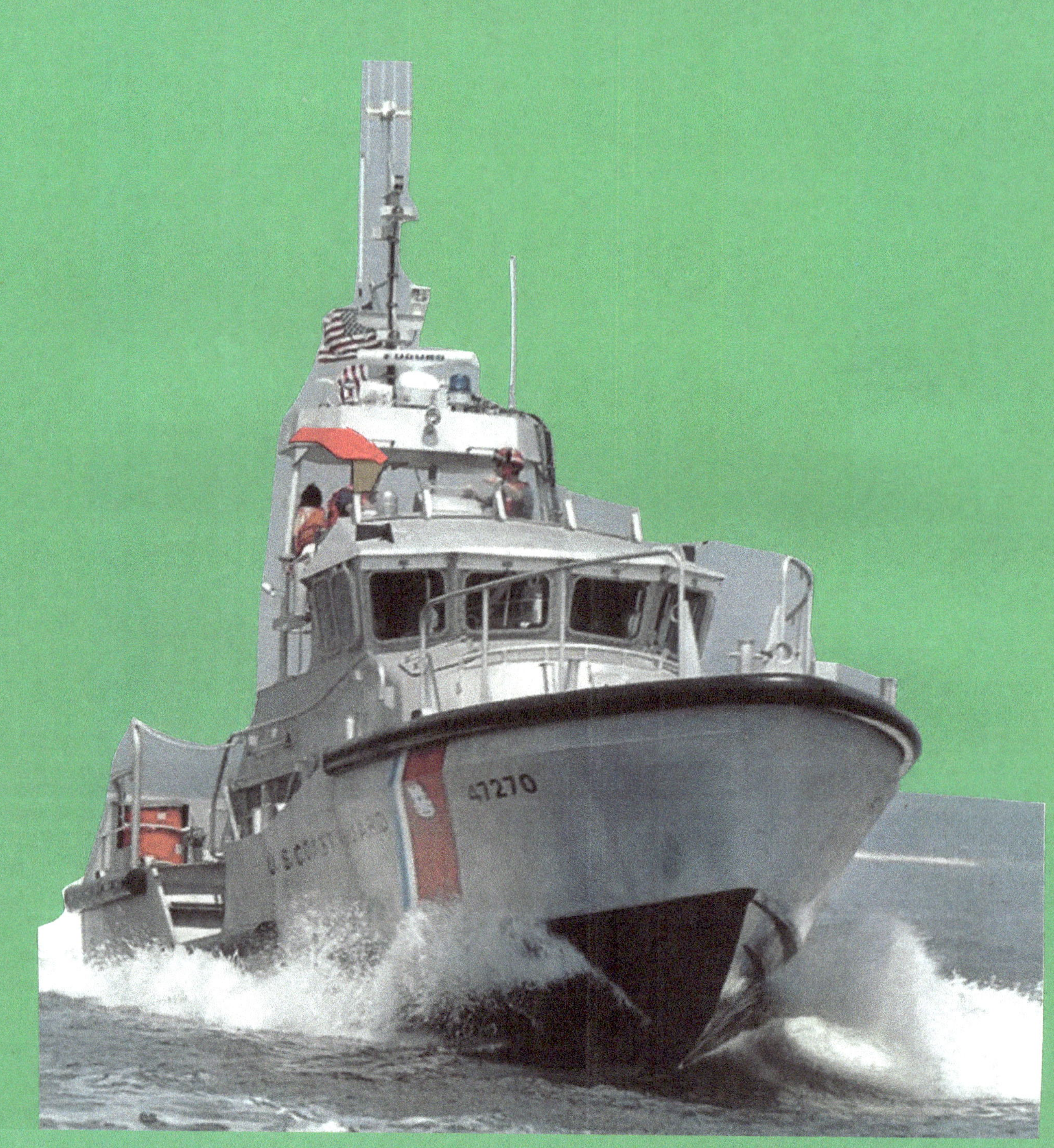

47270
U.S. COAST GUARD

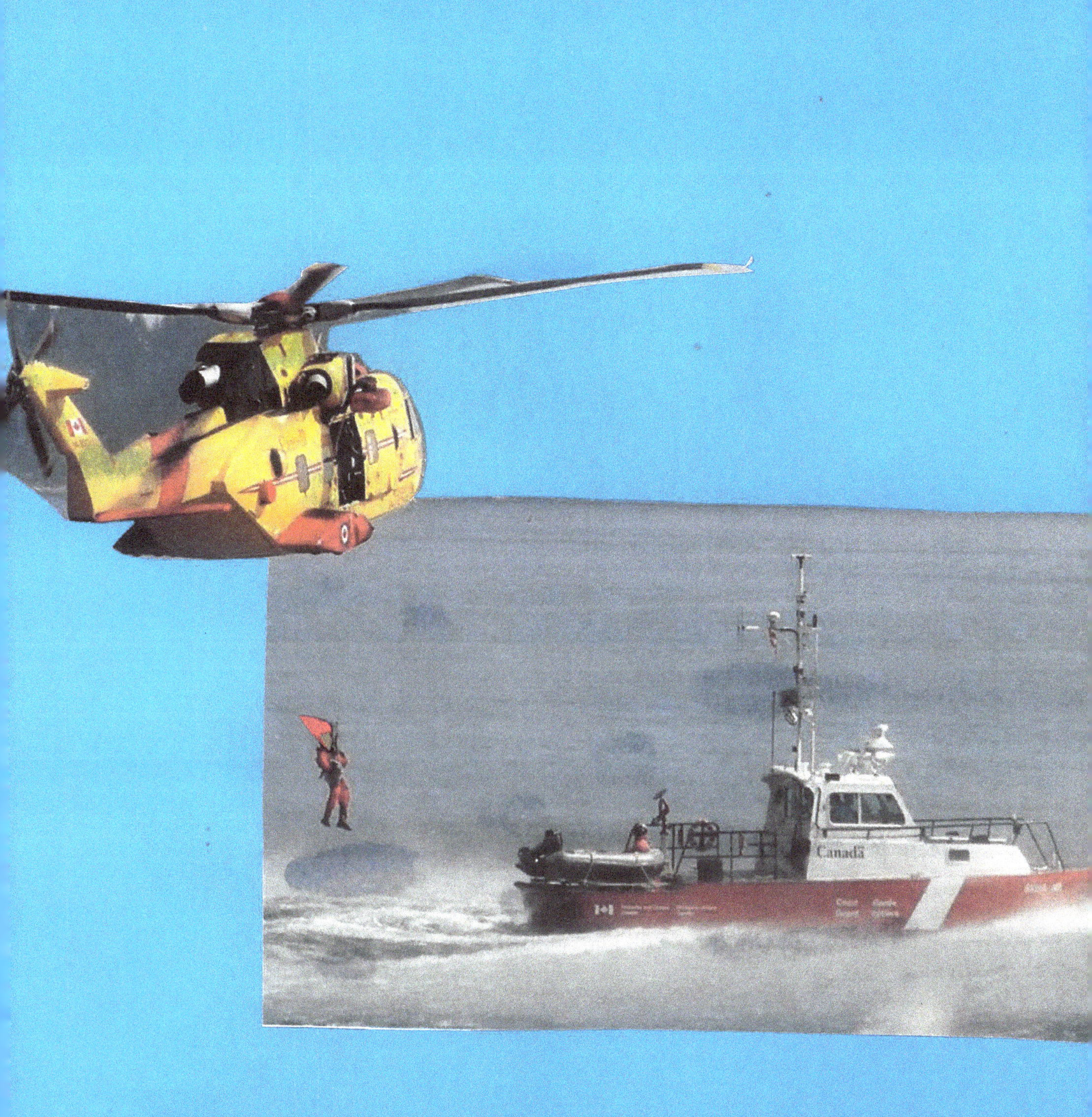

My mom is beautiful and wise,
she brings home the bacon
and eats it with fries.

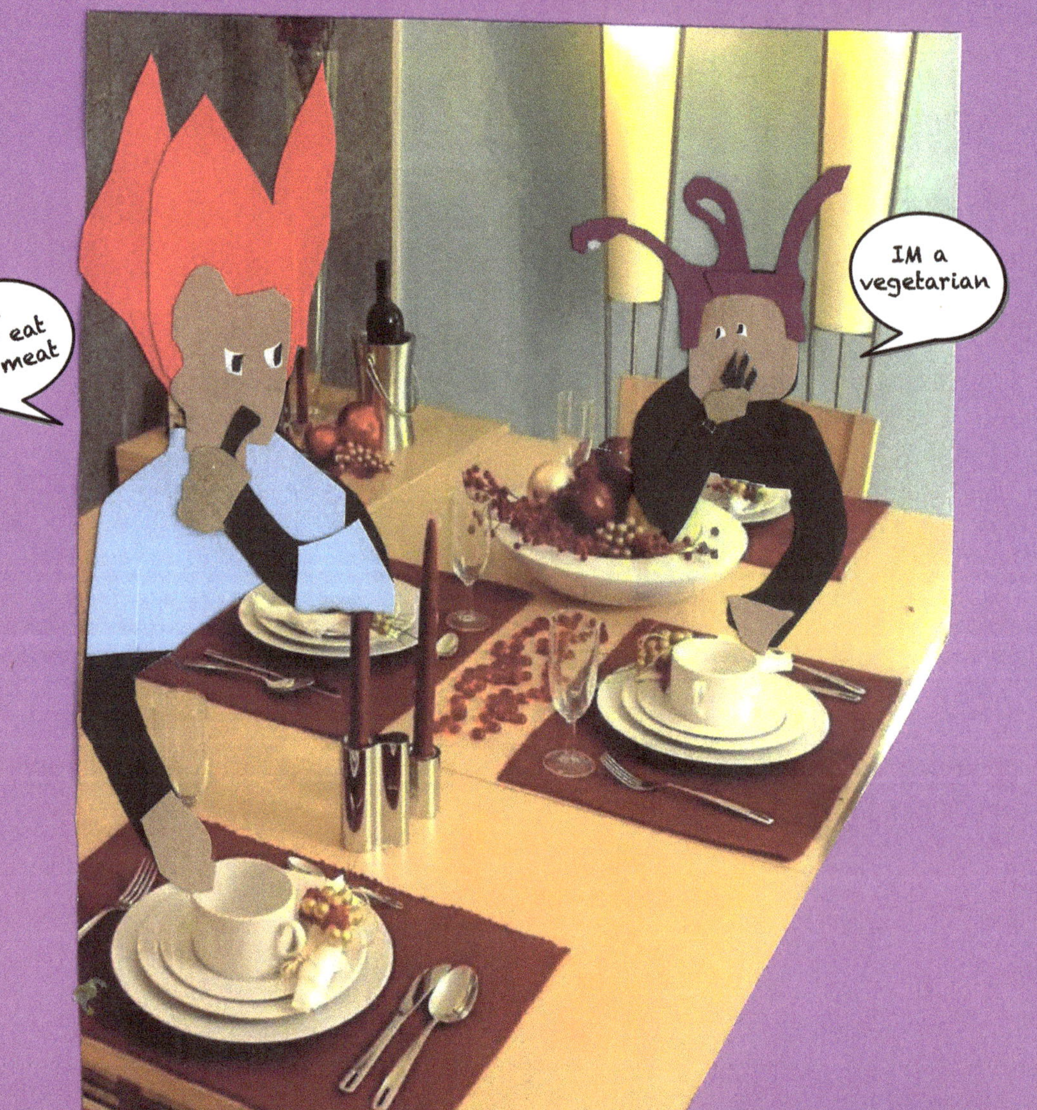

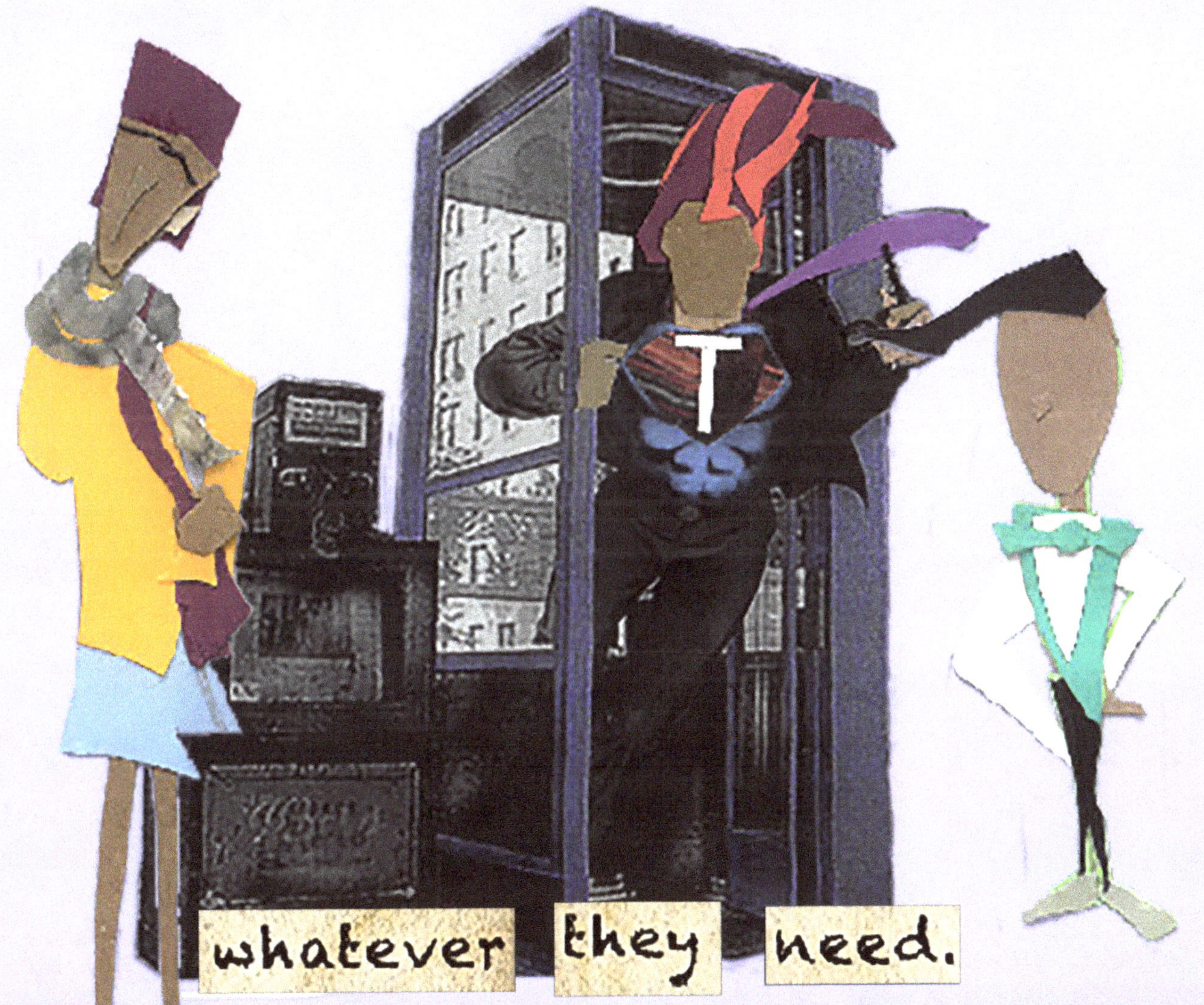
How is this possible?
Evolution indeed.
Humans adapt and transform into
whatever they need.

Thank You,
Mom,
Frances Marie,
you allowed me to be authentic
and showed me the true meaning of love.
R.I.P.

Thank You,
my talented compassionate boys
who help me apply my understanding
of love and stretch me to new limits.

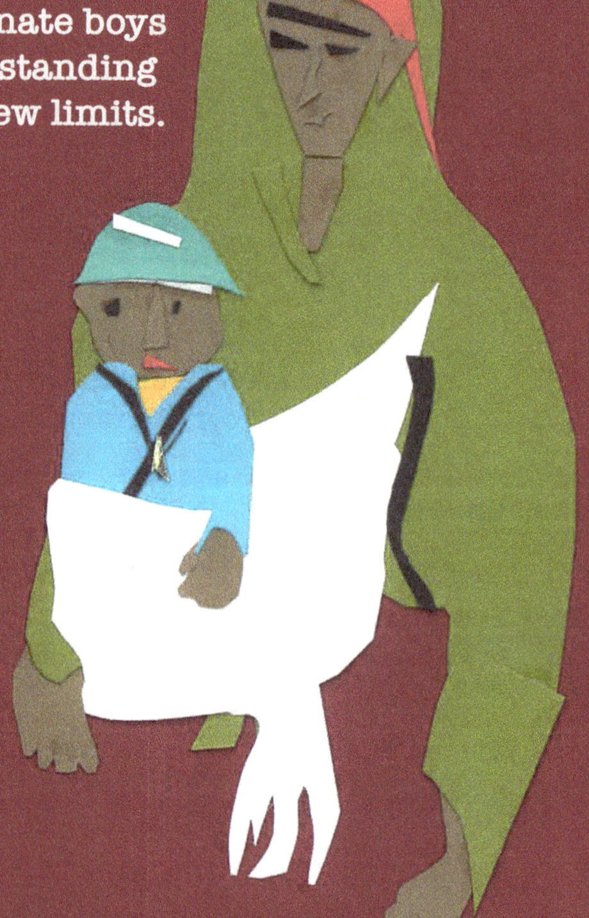